YOU CHOOSE
BOOKS

TOWER OF LONDON

A CHILLING INTERACTIVE ADVENTURE

by Blake Hoena

CAPSTONE PRESS
a capstone imprint

You Choose Books are published by Capstone Press,
1710 Roe Crest Drive, North Mankato, Minnesota 56003
www.mycapstone.com

Library of Congress Cataloging-in-Publication Data
Cataloging-in-Publication data is on file with the Library of Congress.
ISBN 978-1-5157-2579-4 (library binding)
ISBN 978-1-5157-2583-1 (eBook PDF)

Editorial Credits
Mari Bolte, editor; Heidi Thompson, designer; Wanda Winch, media researcher;
Laura Manthe, production specialist

Photo Credits
Alamy: A.P.S. (UK), 104, Mary Evans Picture Library, 89; Bridgeman Images: Private
Collection/Gino D'Achille (20th Century)/The Execution of Anne Boleyn, Illustration
from the "Observer on Sunday", 26; Corbis: Arcaid/English Heritage/H Bedford Lemere,
46, Christie's Images, 78, Jonathan Blair, 19, 33; Courtesy of Lara Eakins, 61; Dreamstime:
Mark Eaton, 100, Rafael Ben-ari, 10; Getty Images: Hulton Archive, 42; Rex Shutterstock:
Colin Davey, 74; Shutterstock: aslysun, cover (tower), Cranach, cover (skull), Cristian
Santinon, 93, Dmitry Naumov, 67, ecco, cover, 1 (clouds), happykanppy, old paper painting
design, IR Stone, 6, 58, italianphoto, cover, 1 (lightning), Jorge Felix, Costa, 12, Manamana,
38, Maria Fedyaeva, 4, pisaphotography, 98, Plateresca, grunge label design, run4it, grunge
paper painting design, saki80, grunge frame design; SuperStock: Heritage, 21, 48, 51, 64,
81, 95

Printed in Canada.
009633F16

Table of Contents

INTRODUCTION

YOU are visiting the historic Tower of London. It's up to you to make the right choices. Will you make it through the haunted castle to see another day? Or will you become part of the Tower's legend? Start by turning the page. The choices you make will change the outcome. After you finish one path, go back and read the others to see how the decisions you make change your fate. Do you have what it takes to make it through the Tower of London?

The Tower of London was first built to scare and awe Londoners into obeying. It was also meant to keep invaders away.

THROUGH THE GATES

Tires screech as your bus grinds to a halt. You look up from your phone and glance out the window. Outside, tourists mill about. In the distance, an old brick wall runs along the horizon. Poking above its battlements, you see the White Tower, the centerpiece of the fortress known as the Tower of London.

You turn to see your best friend, Jerry, waving to you from the front of the bus.

"I have to get my stuff!" you shout back. You grab your jacket off the seat. Fog is starting to roll in; it could be chilly tonight.

"We need to get our tickets at the Welcome Center," Jerry says. "Hurry up." Then he jumps off the bus and disappears.

Turn the page.

You and your friend are here for the twilight tour, which focuses on the weird things that have happened at the Tower. You don't really believe in ghosts. But hearing about supernatural stuff sounded fun.

Once you have your tickets, you and Jerry follow a group through a tower gate. Just on the other side waits a man dressed as a Yeoman Warder, an old-fashioned Royal Guard. The man's red and gold-trimmed uniform, with its large, frilly white collar and black top hat looks funny to you. But you figure his traditional garb is meant to add some authenticity to the tour.

"Welcome to the Tower of London!" the guide says. "Built in 1078 as a fortress, it has also served as a palace, a royal mint, and a prison. There are 21 different towers—13 that frame the complex, and eight inside."

Your guide goes on to tell the tour group about the Royal Menagerie. Past monarchs kept wild animals there for display.

"Rumor has it," your guide continues, "that a ghostly Menagerie member still remains." Some members of your group gasp with excitement.

Your group gathers on a stone bridge. A green lawn stretches out below you. The yeoman tells you that it was once a moat. "The moat was drained by the Duke of Wellington in 1845. Occasionally though, when the Thames River floods, the moat does as well."

You cross over the bridge and then walk through another gate. You're now inside the Tower's outer wall. To your left rises Bell Tower. Ahead is Water Lane, a walkway that leads you to the Tower's main gate. To your right, just on the other side of the outer wall, is the River Thames.

Turn the page.

As you walk, the yeoman tells you pieces of the Tower's history.

"Here is St. Thomas' Tower," he says, motioning to a building that stands between you and the river.

"And this gate here is called Traitors' Gate," he continues. "This gate is so named because so many traitors to the Crown, from Guy Fawkes to Lady Jane Grey, had entered the castle through this gate."

Between two and three million people visit the Tower of London every year.

From where you stand, steps lead down to the wooden gate. "This is a water gate," the guide explains. "There is no water there now. But in the past, pumps controlled the water level so that boats could pass through."

"Those who were executed," your guide continues, "had their heads displayed on poles along London Bridge, just downriver from here."

"Cool," Jerry whispers in your ear. "This is the weird type of stuff I wanted to hear about." You are excited too.

Your group moves on. You enter the inner walls through a gate under a squat, rectangular building that your guide calls the Bloody Tower. Jerry catches your arm and you hang back.

"Let's go down there," your friend says, nodding toward Traitors' Gate.

Turn the page.

"Sure, why not," you say. "We can always catch up with the group."

You cross back through the Bloody Tower and jog down some stairs. Traitors' Gate is made of wooden beams with iron bars running through them. It is sealed shut, but Jerry grabs the bars and shakes them, making loud wailing noises.

You look around, embarrassed and worried that people might see you or hear you. But there is no one near. It seems as though you're alone.

The Traitors' Gate was built in the late 1270s.

As you watch your friend goof off, fog rolls in. Mixed with the grayness of the surrounding castle, the thick haze makes it difficult to see. Ravens caw from above. A chilly wind sweeps over you. You shiver as you zip up your jacket.

"Come on," you say, grabbing Jerry's arm. "We should catch up with the guide."

You don't want to admit to your friend, but you are getting a little creeped out. The sun is setting, casting long shadows over the area, and you don't want to get left behind by your group.

You walk back inside the Tower walls, but you don't see your tour group anywhere. Actually, with the heavy fog, it's difficult to see much of anything. What you can see is the ominous White Tower, straight ahead. The oldest part of the Tower of London, it stands 90 feet tall, rising above even the gray fog.

Turn the page.

"I think the group was headed to Tower Green. Or maybe the Queen's House?" Jerry says, looking around. You can hear how unsure he is.

Tower Green is an open, grassy lawn where several executions took place. The Queen's House is rumored to be one of the castle's most haunted buildings. You know that the tour was making a stop at each place, and they are both close. You just can't remember which one was first. They're both in the same area, at least.

To go to Tower Green, go to page 15.

To go to the Queen's House, turn to page 17.

One of you has to make a decision. "Let's check out Tower Green first," you say.

"Maybe this will help," Jerry says, pulling a map from his pocket. "I grabbed this at the Welcome Center," he explains.

And it's a good thing he did. While you can see hints of buildings, the fog blurs out most identifying features. You know Tower Green is somewhere ahead of you.

"Up there to the left," Jerry says, pointing. He hurries down a stone walkway.

You are quick to run after him. You've already lost track of your tour group. You don't want to lose your friend as well.

In your haste, you plow into Jerry. Your friend has suddenly stopped. You are about to say something when Jerry puts a finger to his lips.

Turn the page.

"Listen," your friend whispers.

You pause. There is an odd sound, coming from your right. *Footsteps?* Yes, marching footsteps. Then you see shadowy figures moving through the fog. You squint, but you can't tell if it's your tour group. *What if it's not?* You could get in trouble just wandering around the castle alone at this time of night. After all, the Crown Jewels are locked up somewhere in the fortress. You don't want anyone to think you're up to no good.

To approach the shadowy figures, turn to page 20.

To avoid the shadowy figures, turn to page 35.

"The Queen's House is to our left," Jerry says, pointing.

From what you know of this building, it's where the Resident Governor lives. He is in charge of the day-to-day operations that happen at the Tower of London.

You follow Jerry. In the fog, you can't see anyone around you. You don't hear anyone either. It's as if you and Jerry are all alone.

Seemingly out of nowhere, you are in front of the white and brown-trimmed Queen's House. Its half-wooden construction makes it seem less aged than the stone buildings around it. You reach out to touch the wall. As you extend your arm, a faint noise catches your attention.

"Now what?" Jerry asks, looking around. "There's no one here."

Turn the page.

"Quiet," you say, hushing your friend. "I thought I heard something."

You hear a whispered name: "William." It drifts in through the fog.

"I think it's coming from inside," Jerry says, looking at the Queen's House.

"William?" the voice, a woman's voice, calls out again.

It's a little louder than before. You think the woman sounds as if she might need help.

You take a step toward the building. There is a door in front of you.

"William?" the voice comes again, sounding more desperate.

You take another step forward, but Jerry grabs your arm.

"We can't go in," your friend says. "Someone actually lives there."

To go in to find the woman, turn to page 23.

To stay outside and look for your tour group, turn to page 35.

Legend says that certain rooms of the Queen's House are off-limits to women. The ghost of the Grey Lady haunts any woman who tries to stay the night.

"That could be our group," you say. "Let's catch up to them."

You jump ahead of Jerry and walk quickly through the thick fog. You start to cross a lawn.

"Hey," you shout. "Hold up!"

You think you hear people, but it doesn't quite sound like tourists. There is none of the usual, nonstop chatter. No one is exchanging tales of adventure or going on excitedly about the sights they have seen—as if they could see anything in this fog. All you hear is rhythmic footsteps. Every footfall is followed by a muffled metal clink.

Then Jerry is by your side. "Look," he says, pointing to the people. "I don't think that's them."

You can see the outline of several yeomens' hats. Your group only had the one guide.

They must be Royal Guards, you think. *I hope we don't get in trouble.*

A woman trails behind the guards. You can't see any clear details through the fog. But she walks proudly despite holding her hands in front of her as if they were bound.

Despite its bloody reputation, only 22 prisoners have ever been executed at the Tower of London.

Turn the page.

The shadowy yeomen lead the woman up a set of steps and onto a platform. Then the woman turns in your direction and begins to speak.

" … I am come hither to die, for according to the law, and by the law I am judged to die … " she says dramatically. It seems to be some kind of prepared speech.

You listen in stunned silence. After she is done, the yeomen force the woman to her knees. She bends forward. Then a tall, dark figure steps out of the fog. He carries a large axe.

"What? This can't be real!" Jerry says. He looks very worried.

To stop the execution, turn to page 25.

To leave, turn to page 33.

You wonder if it's fear that holds your friend back. Jerry seemed brave as he joked around down by Traitors' Gate, but the creepiness of the castle must be getting to him too.

"I don't think there was even a William in our group," Jerry points out.

"How would you even know?" you ask. "Maybe that was our guide's name."

Then you hear the whispered name again.

"It sounds like she might be lost too," you say, pulling away. "We can help each other." You open the door and walk in.

"William?"

You head toward the voice. Through the door and down a hall, you walk. Even inside, the fog casts everything in gray shadow. You walk down a hall, following the sound of the woman's voice.

Turn the page.

Suddenly, you hear a creak behind you. You spin around, your hands raised in front of your face to defend yourself.

"It's just me," Jerry says, stepping out of the fog.

You let out a sigh of relief. The relief is short lived, though.

"William?" the voice says, closer now.

"It sounds like it's coming from that room," Jerry says, pointing. It's a doorway, but the hallway is too dark to see anything.

To go in, turn to page 28.

To make Jerry go first, turn to page 30.

"No way that's real," you tell Jerry. "It's got to be an act."

"Are you sure?" your friend asks. You can tell by the sound of his voice that he is a little freaked out. And you can't blame him.

"Nobody has been executed here since World War II," you say, trying to sound confident. But between the thick fog and the ghastly sight in front of you, you're a little creeped out. You need to find out what's happening. Before you lose your nerve, you dash forward.

"Hey!" you shout. "Is this part of the tour?"

The woman, the guards, and the executioner all turn to you. It's strange—no matter how close you get, their features never become clearer. The fog hides them in its smoky tendrils, as if the people aren't real. A chill runs down your spine.

Turn the page.

Henry VIII sent for a special executioner from France to behead Anne Boleyn. Executions in England were usually done with an axe. Sword cuts were cleaner and thought to be more effective.

You turn, intending to ask Jerry what he sees. But the fog has swallowed your friend. You're about to call out to him when two shadowy yeomen step toward you. Before you can run, they grab your arms. For ghostly figures, their grip is surprisingly strong. They drag you away screaming.

You eventually learn that you interrupted a paranormal reenactment of Queen Anne Boleyn's beheading. For your crime the ghostly yeomen toss you into the White Tower's dungeon. You yell and shout and bang on the cell door, but there's no way out. You are now forever a prisoner in the oldest tower.

In the years to come, these noises spook both visitors and workers alike. Rumors spread of a new ghost haunting the Tower of London: you.

THE END

To follow another path, turn to page 14.
To learn more about the Tower of London, turn to page 101.

You take a step inside the room. "Hello?" you call out. "Do you need help?"

Silence.

You glace around the room, but between the fog and the lack of light, it is difficult to pick out any details. You can just make out the frame of a canopy bed. You take a step toward it.

"Are you lost?" you ask. "We are too. Maybe we can help each other?"

Still no reply.

You turn back to see if Jerry followed you into the room. But he's not behind you. Instead, there is a large shadow looming over you.

"Do you—" you start to ask.

Then you feel tightness around your neck. It's as if someone has wrapped their cold fingers around your throat. You swat at the air, but there's nothing to grab. You struggle to breathe. You gasp for air, but none fills your lungs. Everything turns fuzzy, then black.

What you didn't realize is that you entered the Lennox Room in the Queen's House. Lady Arabella Stuart was imprisoned and died in this room. Mystery surrounded her death. There are rumors that she was strangled. Those rumors, it seems, were true—with Stuart taking out her revenge on you.

THE END

To follow another path, turn to page 14.
To learn more about the Tower of London, turn to page 101.

"Hello?" you call out. You swear the woman's voice was coming from this direction. Yet, there's no one around. At least, you can't see anyone in the darkness. You don't just want to walk into a room uninvited. People actually live here. But no one answers.

"Do you think we should go in?" Jerry asks.

"You first," you say. He takes a few hesitant steps through the doorway.

As you squint into the dark, you see something approaching Jerry from inside the room. It looks like a woman.

"William?" she calls out as she approaches. "Is that you?"

You're so focused on trying to make out the shape that you're surprised when Jerry rushes out of the room so quickly. He bumps you hard, nearly knocking you down.

You meet his eyes. There is a hint of fear in his gaze.

"Let's get out of here!" Jerry shouts, rushing past you.

You're not sure what your friend is so afraid of, or what he saw, but you follow without a second glance back. You race down a hallway and some stairs and are soon out of the Queen's House.

"Wait up!" you shout, out of breath. Jerry is still ahead of you, moving away from the house fast.

"Did you see her?" Jerry asks.

"The woman?" you ask, confused. "Yeah, I saw her, but why did you run? Seriously, slow down!"

"She wasn't real," Jerry says, wide eyed. He doesn't slow down. "She was a ghost."

You scoff at the thought, but Jerry doesn't seem to be joking around.

"Are you sure it wasn't just the Resident Governor's daughter or something?" you ask.

"No, I swear," Jerry says. "She was a ghost. A real ghost."

While you didn't think anything was unusual about the woman, you decide not to tease him about it. He does look scared.

"Come on," you say. "Let's find our tour group before we get even more lost."

Turn to page 40.

You aren't sure what is going on. An execution hasn't happened here since World War II. The Tower isn't even used as a prison anymore. So whatever this is, it has to be an act.

"Probably some sort of reenactment," you guess.

"Maybe they're acting out Queen Anne Boleyn's execution," Jerry says. "She was beheaded at Tower Green."

A view of Wakefield Tower, with the Queen's House and Tower Green on the left and the White Tower on the right.

Turn the page.

"Whatever it is," you say, "it sure looks creepy in the fog."

"Yeah," Jerry agrees. "And the ravens cawing constantly definitely isn't helping."

You see the man with the axe walk toward the women. Still half-hidden by shadows, he seems huge and menacing.

"They're probably just trying to scare people," you say. "I bet it's part of some other tour." You don't remember seeing that in the tour pamphlet, though.

You turn away as the executioner raises his axe. Fake or not, you still don't want to watch.

"Let's get out of here," you say to your friend.

You keep walking forward into the fog. The surroundings are still unfamiliar. But you figure you're bound to bump into your tour group, or at least someone who can guide you in the right direction. You just hope you don't get in trouble for wandering around the grounds alone.

The walls and buildings seem closer than ever. The solid stone makes you feel more secure. Even though they're not guiding you anywhere, their presence assures you're not going to accidently fall into the Thames and drown or wander away from the castle.

There are, however, steps. You stumble down as the terrain changes unexpectedly.

"Ow," you grumble, rubbing your knee. "What's this place?"

Turn the page.

Jerry pulls out the map. You use the light from your phone to read it. Jerry squints and points to the nearest tower.

"If we just came from around here," your friend says, "it could be Beauchamp Tower."

"Was it part of our tour?" you ask.

"Yeah, I think so," Jerry replies. "It was used as a prison, so I'm sure it's haunted."

To go into Beauchamp Tower, go to page 37.

To keep walking around outside, turn to page 40.

You head down the steps without falling this time. There's a doorway at the bottom leading into the tower. The doors are open, and you hear something inside. It sounds like voices.

"Come on," you wave to Jerry. "I hear someone. Maybe our tour group is inside."

Jerry looks unsure. "It's going to be dark soon," he says, skipping down the steps two at a time to join you at the doorway. You check your phone for the time. He's right. The Tower area continues to get creepier and creepier as night settles in. You don't blame your friend for being hesitant after the weird things you've come across so far. But what choice do you really have? You're lost, and unless you find your group, you're not going to get un-lost.

The voices seem a little louder now.

Turn the page.

"Think that's them?" you ask.

"I dunno," Jerry says. "But whoever it is, they're somewhere up above, in the tower."

Although it's dark, you shuffle around and find a set of stairs that go up. You carefully start climbing, keeping a hand on the wall. The walls are rough, covered in graffiti scratched into the stone.

The Tower of London can be a spooky place after dark.

"It sounds like someone is crying," Jerry says the next time you hear the voice.

Near the top of the tower, you look out one of the windows. You see a woman dressed in white out between the wall's battlements on the left side of the tower. It seems odd that anyone would be out there this time of night. She must work here, you think. You refuse to believe anything else.

Just then, you hear sounds again. They're close. And it is definitely a man. He's crying.

To follow the woman out onto the wall, turn to page 42.

To search for the crying man inside the tower, turn to page 45.

"Let's go back to the main entrance," Jerry says. "I'm not sure about this tour anymore."

At this point, you figure you're never going to find your group. Plus, you can tell your friend is more than a little afraid. So that sounds like a good idea. Maybe you can call a cab to pick you up.

You turn back in the direction of the Bloody Tower. This is the way back to the main gate—you think. The echoing of the ravens' caws is messing with your sense of direction. It's dark, and you can't use the moon or the stars as a guide. And even though you have a map, it's not much help when you don't know which buildings are which.

After walking around for a little while, you begin to feel more and more turned around. You catch a glimpse of the domed-top White Tower to your right. But shouldn't it be to your left if you are heading toward the main entrance?

You head in what you think might be the right direction. But you don't take more than a few steps before you hear the sound of people approaching. Their feet make a scraping noise on the stone walkway. Eerily, though, they don't make any other sounds. The sound of cawing from the ravens perched atop one of the towers seems almost ear-splitting in contrast.

You're pretty sure it's not your tour group that's approaching. Regular people would be talking and laughing. But it's a group of people, and it looks like they know where they are going.

To follow the people, turn to page 60.

To head to the White Tower, turn to page 68.

"Who's that?" Jerry asks. "Does she work here?"

"We won't know until we ask," you say. You step through a doorway and out onto the wall's battlements.

"Hello!" you shout. Your voice echoes around you, bouncing off every wall.

Elizabeth I was held at the Tower while her sister, Mary, held the throne. She was allowed to walk along the battlements between Bell and Beauchamp Towers for exercise. These battlements are also known as "Elizabeth's Walk."

The figure doesn't turn or seem to hear you. She continues on the way she was going.

"Quick," Jerry says. "If we don't follow, we'll lose her in the fog."

At a fast walk, you head out onto the wall toward the Bell Tower. This is the same belfry-topped tower you passed by earlier in the night, when you first entered the castle. That means to your right, somewhere in the distance, is where the bus dropped you off. But now all you can see in that direction is a wall of dark gray mist. There are no tourists milling about. No buses. You can't even make out the Welcome Center. It's as if you've entered another world completely.

"She's going into Bell Tower," Jerry says, pulling you from your thoughts.

Turn the page.

You aren't even halfway across the wall, and the woman is at the doorway of Bell Tower. You're afraid you'll lose her once she goes in.

To keep following her into Bell Tower, turn to page 50.

To head back through Beauchamp Tower, turn to page 56.

You wander through the tower, following the noise.

"I don't think it's anyone from our group," Jerry says. "At least I hope no one is so afraid that they're crying."

"You're probably right," you agree.

It sounds like it's just one man. There are no other voices—nobody is trying to soothe the weeping man or help him at all.

You turn a corner and are met with a doorway on your right. You peek in. There's a man inside, facing a wall. He is running his hands over something carved into the stone wall. Between his sobs, you think you hear him mumble the name "Jane."

"Are you okay?" you ask, taking a step into the room. "Sir? Can you hear me?"

Turn the page.

The man turns toward you. He has no face.

You stumble back and a breathy gasp escapes your body. Your body immediately feels cold and shaky. You turn to run. *Where is Jerry? Did he even come into the room?* you wonder.

The door slams shut with a frightening bang. You rush over and pull on the handle, but it seems to be locked. You can't get it to budge.

"Help! Help!" you scream. "Jerry!"

Beauchamp Tower's large size made it ideal for housing prisoners.

No one answers.

You turn back into the room. The weeping has stopped. The man is gone.

Once your courage has returned, you walk over to the wall to see what the ghostly man was looking at.

You're not surprised to see the word "Jane" etched into the stone. *For Lady Jane Grey*, you think. She was queen for just nine days before being imprisoned in the tower by Mary Tudor as a traitor. And if you remember your history correctly, Jane's husband, the weeping man, was Lord Guildford Dudley. He asked to meet with his wife before their executions, but Jane wouldn't see him.

Turn the page.

As you stare at the letters carved into the wall, you watch in horror as they change from "Jane" to your name.

Does that mean I'm now a prisoner? you worry.

Jane was initially found guilty of treason, but Queen Mary was reluctant to put her to death. However, a later revolt planned by Jane's father sealed her fate.

Then you remember Lady Jane Grey's fate. She was tried for treason and sentenced to death.

You rush back to the door and start banging and screaming. Jerry must be near and will hear you. You hold out hope, but no one comes to help.

Much later, a pair of ghostly yeomen enters the room. They drag you out and to Tower Hill, near the Tower. That is where Lady Jane Grey was beheaded.

You suffer the same fate. No one ever finds your body. No one ever finds Jerry. Your ghostly spirit is all that remains to haunt the Tower of London.

THE END

To follow another path, turn to page 14.
To learn more about the Tower of London, turn to page 101.

"Come on!" you shout to Jerry.

You and your friend run across the wall toward Bell Tower. You rush through the doorway just in time to see the woman turn a corner down a hallway. You follow, but it seems like no matter how much you hurry, she is always just ahead of you.

She enters a room, and you follow her in. Finally you are able to get close. She pauses long enough to peer out a window.

"I think that's the ghost of Lady Jane Grey," Jerry gasps in surprise.

You don't really believe in ghosts. But watching the woman, there is something about her that seems unreal. Her clothes move fluidly, yet there is no wind. You can never get a clear glimpse of her face to see what she really looks like.

Then she screams. You and Jerry jump back in fright. Before you can recover, the ghost is gone.

You want to leave the castle, but Jerry wants to see what the ghost saw. You watch him as he looks out the window.

He waves you over. "Look! Come see."

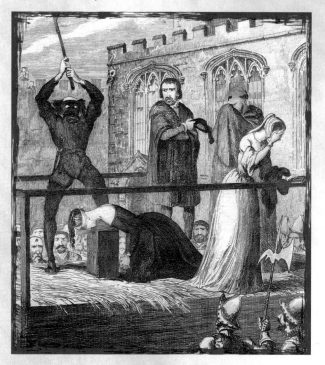

Jane was sentenced to death in November 1553, to "be burned alive on Tower Hill or beheaded as the Queen pleases." She was executed in February 1554.

Turn the page.

Through the fog, you see a group of yeomen leading a horse pulling a cart. Something in the cart looks suspiciously like a headless body.

"I bet that's Jane Grey's husband, Lord Guildford Dudley," Jerry says. "They were both executed for treason."

"How would you know that?" It doesn't matter, but you have to say something. Your heart is still racing. You saw ghosts. Real ghosts!

Jerry smirks and holds up the tour pamphlet.

"I read it when we were waiting for the tour to start," he says. "Now let's get out of here."

To leave through Bell Tower, turn to page 54.

To go back and leave through Beauchamp Tower, turn to page 68.

You figure it's best to leave the way you came. So you and Jerry wind your way through Bell Tower. You find the doorway leading out to the wall.

Partway across the wall, Jerry stops. He looks through the fog to where the bus left you.

"What are you looking for?" you ask.

"Where we got dropped off," your friend says. "That area is Tower Hill. It's where most of the executions took place."

"Yeah, so?" you ask, impatient to leave.

"I was just wondering if we could see what happens to Guildford's ghost from here."

"Seriously?" you say. "I'm out of here!"

Turn the page.

You rush across the wall. You duck through the doorway into Beauchamp Tower. You pause to listen for the weeping man sound you heard earlier. But there's nothing.

"I bet that was Guildford," Jerry says when he catches up to you.

You don't want to think about it. When you close your eyes, you can see the ghostly Guildford being dragged away to be executed. You and Jerry race through the tower's twists and turns until you're back outside.

"Now what?" Jerry asks. "We're still lost."

After the scare you just had, you want to leave. It doesn't matter how.

"Any ideas?" you ask Jerry.

Your friend points toward the White Tower, looming in front of you. In the fog it's just a huge, black shadow. From somewhere up above, a raven's call echoes through the night. You gulp.

"Let's head that way," Jerry says nervously. "There should be a walkway ahead that leads to the main gate."

Turn to page 68.

You grab Jerry and practically drag your friend back into Beauchamp Tower. There was something strange about the woman. Why was she dressed in white when all the other people working here dress in traditional clothing? She looked as though she was floating. You don't want to say it aloud, but you suspect she might have been a ghost.

Once inside the tower, you pause for a moment to listen for the sound of the weeping man. Nothing. You're thankful for that.

You're already a bit scared by the odd things that have been happening to you. Why haven't you seen your tour group yet? Who are the groups of shadowy people who appear and disappear? What are all the strange noises you keep hearing? And on top of that, there's the woman you just saw.

The rumors seem to be true—the Tower of London is truly haunted. And there's more than one ghostly spirit lurking here.

You and Jerry find your way outside. It's almost as dark outside as it was in the old tower. It's hard to know which direction to go. You would have thought there would have been lamps lighting up the grounds. But the only thing you have that can pierce the darkness is the dim light from your phone.

"Where to?" Jerry asks. "Still think we can find our tour group?"

You chuckle nervously. You've given up on that idea. Maybe they left already. Maybe the mist ate them. You don't know. It seems like anything is possible.

"I just hope we can find our way out of here," you admit.

Turn the page.

Jerry pulls out his map. You use your phone to read it. "There's the White Tower, straight ahead," you say. "The Bloody Tower should be somewhere to our right, then. And that's the way out."

You hear a noise and look up. The light from the phone momentarily blinds you. Then out of the fogs steps a procession of people. They march past you.

the entrance through the water gate

"Where did they come from?" Jerry asks, jumping out of their way.

They look like the people you saw earlier at Tower Green. They were reenacting an execution then. You aren't sure what they are doing now. But seeing them a second time gives you hope that they work here.

To follow the procession, turn to page 60.

To head toward the Bloody Tower, turn to page 77.

You aren't sure where the people are going. They're definitely headed away from the exit. But you follow them anyway. Maybe you can ask them for help once they are done with their strange reenactment.

As you walk, Jerry matches your step. He holds up the pamphlet and points to a green spot on the map.

"Scaffold Sight?" you ask, squinting at the paper. "What's that?"

"I think that's where we are," Jerry says.

"Where do you think we're headed?" you ask.

Jerry points to a building marked Chapel of St. Peter ad Vincula. It's just beyond Scaffold Sight.

"A church?" you ask. "Why?" Jerry shrugs.

Three queens—Anne Boleyn, Catherine Howard, and Jane Grey—are buried at the Chapel of St. Peter ad Vincula.

The procession files into to the low gray building. Other people appear and enter too. You follow the tide of people into the church.

Some take seats in the rows of pews. You and Jerry slide into one near the back. Then you notice something odd at the front of the procession.

"Look!" you say, loud enough for people around you to hear. But Jerry is the only one who reacts.

Turn the page.

A figure in regal dress rises from the front of the church. You're sure it's the woman you saw earlier at the Tower Green—the one who was about to be executed. The dress and robes are the same. Only now, she doesn't have her head.

To flee, go to page 63.

To stay, turn to page 65.

You and Jerry practically crawl over each other trying to get out of your seats. You make so much noise that people from the procession turn to watch you. None of the people have faces. They are all ghosts!

You and Jerry can barely stifle your screams. Your legs wobble, but you will them to move. You rush for the doors in the back of the chapel. But before you can reach them, they slam shut.

A violent gust of wind from the front of the church makes you turn. The headless woman storms down the aisle toward you. You back up against the doors as she reaches you. You raise your hands in front of your face in fear.

Then all goes black.

Turn the page.

The church that first stood at the Chapel of St. Peter ad Vincula was built even before the White Tower. The chapel has been rebuilt several times over the centuries.

Sometime later, you and Jerry find yourself seated in one of the pews. Neither of you can move. You are stuck where you sit. You had interrupted Anne Boleyn's funeral procession. As punishment, you are now forced to join the hallowed march. Every night, for the rest of eternity, you make your way to the Chapel to witness her burial.

THE END

To follow another path, turn to page 14.
To learn more about the Tower of London, turn to page 101.

Every muscle in your body wants you to get up and leave. Instinct tells you that you need to run for your life. But you realize that you are in the middle of a funeral procession. You don't dare disrupt such a holy event. You worry what might happen if you do.

Turning to Jerry, you put a finger to your lips. You see the fear in your friend's eyes, but he nods back.

Looking more closely at the people filing into the chapel, you start to notice something odd about them. Their clothes are ghostly white. No matter how hard you stare, you can't get a clear view of anyone's face. And apart from a light shuffle, they make no noise. Nobody coughs or sneezes or even breathes aloud.

Turn the page.

As you sit there, watching, you piece things together. Earlier, at Tower Green, you saw what you had thought was a reenactment of an execution. It must have been Anne Boleyn's. She was beheaded there. Could this be her funeral procession? You know she was buried here.

You watch as the headless figure floats up to the altar. When she reaches the front of the church, she turns to the shadowy figures gathered.

Then, in a blink of the eye, she is gone. With her, all the other ghostly figures have disappeared too.

What you just witnessed was probably the scariest thing you've ever seen in your life. "Whoa," you whisper.

"Let's get out of here," Jerry says.

You slowly rise from your seat. Still fearful of what might happen, you quietly creep to the door and pull it open. Then you dive once more into the fog and darkness.

You find the White Tower in the distance and walk toward it, fixating on its domed roof like it's a beacon. It stands in the middle of the Tower of London. It's the best landmark you could have to help you figure out where to go.

The basement of the White Tower was once used as a torture site.

Turn the page.

Jerry stays close. After what you've seen, every little sound causes both of you to jump in fear. And the night is no longer empty and gray. It now seems alive with noises. You hear soldiers marching across the ground but see no one. Ravens croak and caw from above. The wind swirls about, creating smoky eddies of fog. There are mysterious screams in the distance.

You reach the White Tower. You circle it, trying to find the side that faces Bloody Tower, the way to the exit. You find steps that lead to a door. You reach for the handle when you hear a growl from somewhere in the darkened fog.

You recall earlier when your tour guide mentioned that a ghostly animal from the Royal Menagerie roams the grounds. The last thing you want to do is run into a ghost bear or lion.

You wonder if you can escape past the Bloody Tower's exit before it finds you. Maybe it would be better to find a safe spot to stay inside the White Tower.

To hide inside the White Tower, turn to 71.

To run for the exit, turn to page 77.

The growl is louder now. Jerry pushes you toward the White Tower.

"Are you sure about this?" you ask. You can see the fear in your friend's eyes, but he nods.

You aren't sure, though. After all that you've seen, is inside another tower really any safer than outside? You enter the door to the tower anyway.

You don't get very far before something tickles your ear. It's nothing more than a whisper, but you hear it. "There's just us here," it says.

"What do you think that means?" Jerry asks. His voice is one step below a shriek.

You don't know, and you don't want to stick around to find out. You and Jerry run. In the darkness, you aren't sure where you are going. You weave in and out of pillars and around furniture. Eventually you find a staircase and follow it up.

By the time you calm down, you are totally lost. You pause to catch your breath—just in time to spot a shadowy figure rounding a corner.

After all you've been through tonight, you can't tell if it's a real person or another ghostly spirit. You don't want to wait around to find which one it is.

You turn to run, pulling Jerry along with you. As you go, you hear the figure turn. Then it starts stomping behind you.

In your flight, you pass by several rooms. Maybe you should duck into one of them and hide.

To duck into a room that look likes it might have been a prison cell, turn to page 72.

To duck into a room full of old armor, turn to page 74.

You and Jerry duck into a small stone room to escape whoever—or whatever—is following you down the hallway. The room doesn't have any furnishings. Where will you hide?

A ghostly woman in white suddenly appears in front of you. She's looking out a window and waving. She doesn't appear to see you.

"Who ... who is that?" you ask. Jerry shakes his head.

Just as you think about leaving the room, the loud footsteps pass by. You need to remain hidden. The ghostly woman in front of you doesn't seem nearly as frightening.

You brave a few steps forward. Standing on your toes, you can just see past the woman and through the window. You see two boys through the fog. They've stopped their play and are waving back at the woman.

"Don't mess around," Jerry whispers, pulling you back. "We don't want her to know we're here."

Of all the strange things you've seen tonight, this white woman seems harmless, almost sad.

"It's OK," you say. "I feel like we're OK."

Jerry peeks through the doorway.

"Whatever was out there is gone," he says. "Let's go before it comes back."

With a final glance at the white woman, you leave the room. You and Jerry wind your way out of the White Tower.

Turn to page 77.

You step into a large gallery. Suits of armor line the walls. The most impressive-looking armor is right in front of you. It's huge and shiny. The plaque tells you the armor belonged to King Henry VIII.

"Wow, he was king-sized," you say, stepping forward to get a better look.

Henry VIII's armor weighed more than 50 pounds (22.7 kilograms).

Suddenly everything goes black. It feels as if a thick, heavy cloak has been thrown over you. You squirm and try to free yourself from its weight, but you can't toss the covering off.

A crushing grip smothers you. It squeezes you from all sides. You want to scream. But you can't. You can't even breathe.

You faint, collapsing to the ground.

When you wake, you find yourself in a small, dark prison cell with no windows. As you stand up, you bump your head against the ceiling. You have to crouch to walk the few steps to the cell's wooden door.

No matter how hard you bang against it, it won't open.

Turn the page.

"Help!" you scream. You yell until your voice grows rough and raspy. You bang and kick at the door, but it never moves. There is no way out for you.

Your pleas for help now haunt a cell in the White Tower's dungeon known as "Little Ease". You've just become another one of the castle's many ghosts.

THE END

To follow another path, turn to page 14.
To learn more about the Tower of London, turn to page 101.

You stumble blindly until you find yourself standing in front of Bloody Tower.

Finally, you think. This is the way out.

The sound of giggling draws your attention away from the gate. You look to your left and see two boys watching you. They are dressed in white nightshirts.

For a second you wonder what two boys would be doing out here in the middle of the night. Then it dawns on you. They can't be real. They have to be ghosts. Next to you, you hear Jerry gasp.

"It's them," your friend says. "It's the Princes in the Tower. Those are the ghosts of princes Edward and Richard."

Turn the page.

Edward V traveled to the Tower of London expecting to attend his coronation. Instead he entered his prison. His brother, Richard, joined him shortly after.

Even you've heard of these ghosts. The boys went into the Tower of London as prisoners and never came out. Some say their uncle, the Duke of Gloucester, ordered their imprisonment so he could take the crown in Edward's place. Others say the Duke was responsible for the princes' deaths too. The boys' bodies were never found.

You realize the giggling has stopped. Instead, a low growl echoes throughout the night.

You glance back at the boys. They look afraid and motion you toward them.

"I think they want us to follow them," you say to Jerry.

To leave through the gate, turn to page 80.

To follow the princes, turn to page 83.

"I don't care what they want," Jerry says. "They aren't real. But we are, and we need to get out of here."

You notice your friend's voice is fearful and high pitched. Jerry is deathly afraid. You understand. You're struggling to stay calm yourself. Then you hear another growl, and your whole body seems to shake from the inside out.

"Come on!" Jerry shouts.

Your friend pulls you toward the exit. You're nearly to the water walkway, which will lead you to Byward Tower and across the bridge to where you first joined your tour. The start of the tour seems like a far-off memory.

You're jolted back to reality when a dark, lumbering shadow blocks your path. At first you think it might be the shadow from a tree or part of a building. But then the shadow growls.

The shadow takes a step toward you and Jerry. *Reminds me of a bear*, you think, dazed. But there are no bears in Great Britain. That's your last coherent thought.

Legend says that the "grizzly ghost" scared one guard so badly that he dropped dead from shock.

Turn the page.

You turn to run, but it doesn't matter. A huge, brutish paw easily brings you down. There is no way either you or Jerry can outrun the ghostly bear that haunts what once was part of the Tower's Royal Menagerie.

THE END

To follow another path, turn to page 14.
To learn more about the Tower of London, turn to page 101.

"Wait a second," you say to Jerry. You hear your friend's exasperated sigh as he stops.

"Come on," you plead. "I think they want to help us."

"They probably just want to show us where their bodies are buried," Jerry mutters. You pretend not to hear him. You want to see where the boys lead you. But as you step toward them, they back away.

"Wait!" you yell as you rush to keep up. They lead you to the Bloody Tower. As you take your next step forward, they disappear through a door.

"Great, they're gone," Jerry says. "Can we go now?"

He's answered with a loud growl. It's close—maybe just on the other side of the Bloody Tower's gate.

Turn the page.

"Remember that ghostly animal the tour guide mentioned?" you ask.

Jerry gulps nervously and nods.

"I … I think that's it," you stammer.

To take your chances outside, go to page 85.

To follow the princes, turn to page 87.

"Let's not go into another haunted tower," Jerry pleads. "Those boys are probably in there waiting. Who knows what they have in mind for us?"

You're not so sure that they were out to get you. But Jerry's concern is valid. Every other place you've gone into has been haunted in one way or another. There probably are ghosts inside.

But there also seems to be a ghost outside. More growls from behind the gate make you second-guess your choice not to go in.

You slowly back away from the gate and head back toward Tower Green, where your scary night began. But at least that part of the grounds is familiar to you.

Turn the page.

The growls fade the farther you get from the Bloody Tower. Maybe whatever it was has moved on, you hope.

"I'm not sure we're ever getting out of he—" Jerry says when you reach the edge of the Tower Green.

He's interrupted by a chilling scream. A ghostly woman comes rushing out of the dark fog, wailing as she races past you. You can see she has a shoulder injury. Silvery ghost blood drips from the wound.

To get away from the ghost, turn to page 89.

To run the same way as the ghost, turn to page 91.

The two ghostly princes seem much less threatening than whatever waits outside. Determined, you enter the Bloody Tower. As you wander, the princes' voices echo all around you. Sometimes they laugh and play. Other times they cry and whimper. They lead you on until you are lost within the tower.

A dim light shines through a doorway ahead. Outside of your phone, it's the first actual light you've seen since your adventure began.

Peeking around its frame, you see a well-furnished room. A man sits behind a desk. He seems well dressed in old-fashioned but high-quality clothing. He looks at a map and appears to be taking notes in a journal.

"Well, come in," he says when he sees you. "It's been ages since anyone has visited me."

Turn the page.

You aren't quite sure what to make of the man. But he at least seems friendly.

"Maybe he can help us," Jerry whispers.

In the distance, you hear the boys shriek.

To enter the room, turn to 95.

To wait to see what the man does first, turn to 97.

After all you've seen tonight, you decide it's best to go the opposite direction. That means heading away from the main gate—but also away from the screaming ghost.

You can hear the woman scream a few more times in the distance. Then, mid-scream, she goes silent. You hear nothing but the rustling wind and the constant cawing of ravens.

Margaret Pole was the last of her royal line, the Plantagenets.

Turn the page.

"What do you think she was running from?" Jerry asks.

"I don't know," you shrug. "I guess she wasn't in the pamphlet?" Jerry shakes his head and scowls at you but doesn't respond.

What would a ghost be afraid of? you wonder.

Then fear washes over you as you realize that anything scaring a ghost is probably something you should be afraid of too. The crunch of a foot on gravel causes you to turn. Your eye catches the glint of metal—an axe, raised as if to strike.

Your scream is cut off—along with your head.

THE END

To follow another path, turn to page 14.
To learn more about the Tower of London, turn to page 101.

On the one hand, running after a strange ghost—especially after what you've already seen tonight—seems crazy. On the other hand, the thing scaring her has to be incredibly frightening too. Maybe the best thing to do is to follow her.

You let the ghost lead you. She circles the Tower Green, bringing you close to the Bloody Tower once again. Then, suddenly, she crumbles to the ground as if struck, and disappears.

But you don't stop. You keep running. You dash through the Bloody Tower's gates. You take a right, running toward the exit. You hear a loud growl behind you, but you don't look back. Ravens caw after you. The fog swirls.

Bell Tower flashes by on the right. Byward Tower is ahead. You can see the tower's gate—the way out.

Turn the page.

You don't hesitate. You dash through.

All of a sudden, the fog seems to magically disappear, as if you suddenly entered another world. The real world.

You and Jerry stop, bent over and gasping for air. When you finally look up, you see a group of people just in front of you. It's your tour group. They were chatting amongst themselves but had stopped upon spotting you and Jerry. The tour guide coughs to get everyone's attention and continues his lecture as though nothing has happened.

"And as I was saying," he says, "Margaret Pole was the niece of Edward IV, father to the Princes in the Tower. People have seen Margaret's ghost running across Tower Green as she tries to escape her executioner. But in truth, that never happened ..."

As the group leaves the Tower of London, the tourists chat excitedly about all they had seen tonight.

"It was so cool to see the tower ravens in real life!" one exclaims.

"How grand the Royal Menagerie must have been, full of exotic animals," another says.

Old stories say that if the six ravens who live at the Tower ever leave, the kingdom will fall. Today seven ravens call the Tower of London home.

Turn the page.

"The list of executed people at the Tower Green was fascinating," a woman tells her friend. "How amazing would it have been to really be there?"

You and Jerry share a knowing glance. Nothing your tour group mentions compares to what you have seen tonight.

"Do you think any of them would believe us if we told them what we saw?" Jerry asks when you reach the Welcome Center, where your bus is waiting.

You shake your head as you get on the bus.

THE END

To follow another path, turn to page 14.
To learn more about the Tower of London, turn to page 101.

You enter the room, hoping the man can help you finally get out of this haunted nightmare.

The man shuffles some papers. "I've been planning another trip to El Dorado," he says. "This one will be a success."

"The city of gold?" you ask, confused.

Sir Walter Raleigh founded the first English colony in the New World in 1585.

Turn the page.

"You have heard of it?" he asks. "Then you know where it is!" He sweeps toward you. You see that he has no face. His appearance shimmers as you look at him. Too late you realize he too is a ghost.

Then the door slams shut behind you. You are now locked in the prison cell of Sir Walter Raleigh.

Raleigh was locked up at the Tower for many years. He was released once, then imprisoned again and executed after a failure to find the mythical city of El Dorado. Now you have become his ghostly companions, forever trapped until he finds the fabled lost city of gold.

THE END

To follow another path, turn to page 14.
To learn more about the Tower of London, turn to page 101.

You've entered too many rooms and seen too many ghosts tonight to just rush in. You hesitate outside the doorway.

The man closes his journal and turns to you. He has no face. "Come, join me," he says, beckoning. "We will both be rich when we find the lost city of El Dorado." His ghostly features shimmer in the dim light.

"Let's get out of here," Jerry screams, tugging at your sleeve.

The both of you run, the sound of laughing boys echoing off the walls. After terrifying dead ends and multiple doors, you finally escape the tower.

"The main entrance is this way," Jerry says. You run to the right, and sure enough, there is a gate leading out. Another right, and you are running down Water Lane.

Turn the page.

Byward Tower rises up in front of you, its gate offering safety. You leap through. And as you do, the fog disappears and you see the light from several lamps glowing. It's as if you are suddenly back in the real world.

To your surprise, your tour group is gathered right in front of you. Nobody is looking your direction, and nobody seems to notice your sudden presence.

The last execution at the Tower occurred in 1941.

" … Sir Walter Raleigh had the longest stay of any of the Tower's prisoners," the guide says. "He never did find El Dorado, the fabled city of gold. After his eventual execution, legend says his spirit came to haunt the Bloody Tower."

Jerry turns to you. "So that's who we just saw," he says.

On the way out of the Tower, people talk about all they have heard and seen on the tour. But you and Jerry don't feel you missed out on anything. You experienced more than what anyone on a haunted tour would want to.

"I bet no one would believe us," Jerry says.

"Never," you say, shaking your head. Then you get on the bus, thankful to have survived.

THE END

To follow another path, turn to page 14.
To learn more about the Tower of London, turn to page 101.

EPILOGUE: THE TOWER OF LONDON

The Tower of London has seen kings and lords rise and fall in its nearly thousand-year history. In 1066 William the Conqueror won his claim to England's throne during the Battle of Hastings. He went on to unite England.

The Tower of London spans over 18 acres (7.3 hectares) of land.

During his reign William began building the White Tower near the River Thames. The imposing keep not only protected London, but it was also meant to frighten the people of England into submission. William did not want anyone questioning his right to rule.

Over hundreds of years, the single tower grew into the fortress that is now known as the Tower of London. Smaller towers were built and connected by protective walls called battlements. A moat was dug around the structure. Other buildings, including the Queen's House and Chapel Royal, were added too.

The Tower of London has been used as the seat of government. But it was also a place of misery and pain. Prisoners, mostly traitors to the crown, were tortured. Some were executed. The Tower of London is considered one of the most haunted places in the world.

Various paranormal activities have been reported at Her Majesty's Royal Palace. People claim to have seen ghostly soldiers marching around the grounds. Mysterious footsteps have been heard in several of the buildings. Past kings and queens are said to wander the hallways of certain buildings. The ghostly White Woman has been seen waving from a window in the White Tower. Countess Margaret Pole is rumored to have run screaming across Tower Green trying to escape the executioner's axe.

Perhaps the Tower's most active and well-known ghost is Anne Boleyn, the second wife of King Henry VIII. Henry ended their marriage when it looked as though he would never have a son with Anne. He used treason as an excuse to put her to death. Her ghost is often seen at the place of her execution, the Tower Green, and her place of burial, the Chapel Royal.

Lady Arabella Stuart was born royal, but unlucky. Although she didn't want to be queen, her cousin, King James I, saw her as a threat. When she married against his wishes, he had her imprisoned in the Queen's House for treason. Most stories say she died of an illness, but there are also rumors that she was strangled in her room. Some say her ghost never left.

When King Edward VI died in 1553, his cousin, Lady Jane Grey, was made queen. But her rule lasted for only nine days. Edward's sister took back the crown and imprisoned Jane and her husband Lord Guildford Dudley. They were executed on the same day. Guildford has been heard weeping in Beauchamp Tower. Jane has been seen upon the battlements.

The Princes in the Tower are another tragic tale. Richard and Edward were just boys when their father, King Edward IV, died. Their uncle, the Duke of Gloucester, was charged with looking after the boys until Edward could rule. But the duke claimed the throne for himself and locked the boys in the Tower. They were never seen again.

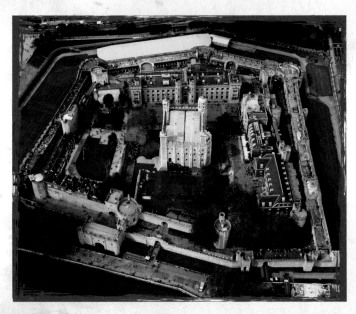

Today the Tower is home to about 150 people, with millions of outsiders visiting every year.

Some believe the princes were able to escape. Many more believe their uncle ordered their murder. Their ghosts have reportedly been seen in both the White and the Bloody Towers.

Today the Tower of London is mostly a museum and a tourist attraction. The fortress attracts visitors from all over the world. Many come to hear about its centuries-old history and to see the Crown Jewels, valuables worn by past rulers. But some come to see the ghosts left behind by the Tower's gruesome history.

TIMELINE

1066—William the Conqueror begins building the Tower of London.

1080s—Construction on the White Tower begins.

1100—Ranulf Flambard, the Tower's first prisoner, is locked up. Six months later, he escapes, becoming the Tower's first prisoner to escape.

1210—The first wild animals—lions—are kept at the Tower.

1272–1307—Edward I reigns. Edward builds the outer defenses of the Tower, making it England's largest and strongest defendable castle.

1278—The Royal Mint is moved to the Tower.

1455–1485—The War of the Roses between the Houses of Lancaster and York is fought.

1483—Edward V and his brother Richard—the Princes in the Tower—disappear and are never seen again.

early 1500s—Construction begins on the version of Chapel of St. Peter ad Vincula that stands today.

1509–1547—Henry VIII reigns. He marries six times, executing two of his wives and divorcing two others. He also builds the Queen's House.

May 15, 1536—Anne Boleyn is beheaded on Tower Hill.

May 27, 1541—Margaret Pole is executed.

1554—Lady Jane Grey and her husband, Lord Guildford Dudley, are executed.

1590s—The first guided tours of the Tower are given to upper-class members who can pay.

September 25, 1615—After months of imprisonment, Arabella Stuart dies.

April 9, 1747—Simon Fraser, the 11th Lord Lovat, is the last man beheaded on Tower Hill.

1811—A grizzly bear named Martin arrives at the Royal Menagerie as a gift to George III. It is the first grizzly bear ever seen in London.

1832—Animals are no longer kept at the Tower. Any remaining animals are sent to the London Zoo.

1845—The Duke of Wellington drains the moat.

1876—The Chapel of St. Peter ad Vincula is renovated, revealing the graves of Anne Boleyn, Catherine Howard, and Lady Jane Grey.

1941—Josef Jakobs is executed. His is the last execution at the Tower.

2008—Renovations on the White Tower begin.

GLOSSARY

altar (AWL-tuhr)—a table or flat-topped surface used for a religious ritual

battlements (BA-tuhl-MENT)—protected walls on the top of a fort or castle with regularly-spaced, square-shaped openings

beacon (BEE-kuhn)—a light or other visible object that serves as a signal or guide

chapel (CHAP-uhl)—a small building used for religious services

El Dorado (EL doh-RAH-doh)—a mythical city of amazing wealth

fortress (FOR-truss)—a military stronghold

garb (GARB)—clothing or dress

hallowed (HAL-ohd)—sacred or respected

menagerie (muh-NA-JUR-ee)—a place where animals are kept and trained

mint (MINT)—a place where coins are made

monarch (MON-urk)—a ruler, such as a king or queen, who often inherits his or her position

ominous (OM-uh-nuhss)—describes something that gives the impression that something bad is going to happen

paranormal (pair-uh-NOR-muhl)—having to do with an unexplained event that has no scientific explanation

reenactment (RE-uhn-ACT-mehnt)—to repeat the actions of an event

renovate (REH-no-vate)—to restore something to good condition

scaffold (SKAF-old)—a temporary or moveable structure on which criminals are killed by being hanged or beheaded

supernatural (soo-pur-NACH-ur-uhl)—something that cannot be given an ordinary explanation

traitor (TRAY-tuhr)—someone who aids the enemy of his of her country

treason (TREE-zuhn)—the crime of betraying your country

twilight (TWYE-liyte)—the time of day when the sun has just set and it's beginning to get dark

yeoman (YO-mehn)—an attendant or officer in a royal or noble household

OTHER PATHS TO EXPLORE

In this book you've seen how terrifying being alone in a haunted place can be. But haunted places can mean different things to different people. Seeing an experience from many points of view is an important part of understanding it.

Here are a few ideas for other haunted points of view to explore:

- The Tower of London has nearly a millennium of dark history behind it. Imagine you're a ghost hunter visiting the Tower. What kinds of ghosts would you seek out? What kind of equipment would you bring?

- What would it have been like to be locked up in the Tower of London? Your fate and how long you might have to stay are unknown. What would this have been like? Would you be afraid? Or would you try to make the best of things?

- For another perspective, what if someone you knew was locked in the Tower instead? Would you visit them, or even try to help them escape? Or would you leave them there alone?

READ MORE

Claybourne, Anna. *All about Henry VIII.* Chicago: Raintree Fusion, 2015.

Nelson, Drew. *Haunted! The Tower of London.* New York: Gareth Stevens Publishing, 2013.

Pipe, Jim. *Dirty Rotten Rulers: History's Villains & Their Dastardly Deeds.* Berkeley Heights, N.J.: Enslow Elementary, 2014.

INTERNET SITES

Use FactHound to find Internet sites related to this book. All of the sites on FactHound have been researched by our staff.

Here's all you do:
Visit *www.facthound.com*
Type in this code: 9781515725794

INDEX